NOV 3 0 2006

D0956011

HANDLING

WHAT TO DO WHEN PEOPLE

DIFFICULT

TRY TO PUSH YOUR BUTTONS

PEOPLE

3 9075 03487864 2

HANDLING

WHAT TO DO WHEN PEOPLE

DIFFICULT

TRY TO PUSH YOUR BUTTONS

PEOPLE

DR. JOHN TOWNSEND

INTEGRITY
HOUSE™
Nashville, Tennessee

Handling Difficult People
By John Townsend

Copyright © 2006 by John Townsend

Published by Integrity House, a Division of Integrity Media, Inc.
660 Bakers Bridge Avenue, Suite 200, Franklin, Tennessee 37067.

Helping people worldwide experience the manifest presence of God.

Published in association with Yates & Yates, LLP Attorneys and Literary Agents,
Orange, California.

All rights reserved. No portion of this book may be reproduced, stored in a retrieval
system, or transmitted in any form or by any means—electronic, mechanical,
photocopy, recording or any other—except for brief quotations in printed reviews,
without the prior written permission of the publisher.

Unless otherwise indicated, Scripture quotations used in this book are from the New
International Version. Copyright © 1973, 1978, 1984 by International Bible Society.
Used by permission of Zondervan Publishing House. All rights reserved.

Cover Design: Wes Youssi | www.thedesignworksgroup.com
Interior: VisibilityCreative.com

ISBN 10 1-59145-477-8
ISBN 13 978-1-59145-477-9

Printed in the United States of America
06 07 08 09 LBM 5 4 3 2 1

Contents

Introduction
A Reality Checklist

A re you in a relationship with someone that often results in you feeling significant amounts of the following? (In your mind, check all that apply.)

- [ ] Frustration
- [ ] Helplessness
- [ ] Fear
- [ ] Alienation and isolation
- [ ] Anxiety
- [ ] A sense that things are out of control
- [ ] A feeling of being unloved
- [ ] Guilt
- [ ] Confusion
- [ ] Anger

If you have a lot of check marks—or even a single check mark that weighs heavily and often on your mind, then this book is for you. Though the reactions listed above don't create a complete checklist of warning signals, they are representative of the kinds of feelings that indicate there is an unhealthy dynamic in an important relationship in your life that is causing significant problems for you, and perhaps for others.

It's certainly possible that these reactions may say more about your own style of relating to others than about the other person. But if it's true, in objective reality, that there is an important person in your life doing lots of crazy-making or even destructive things, then you need help dealing with a button-pusher.

My hope and prayer for this book is that you will begin to find the resources to not only understand your situation, but to also develop an approach to the relationship that both influences that difficult person to change in positive ways and helps you change and grow also.

Will it be easy? Change rarely is. But change is possible whenever we embrace principles that flow out of God's character, grace, and words. It is then that we begin to become the growing person who can positively influence people and relationships.

If you're going to "handle" that difficult person in your life, the time to start is now.

CHAPTER 1
BE HONEST ABOUT LIFE WITH DIFFICULT PEOPLE

God has been in the business of changing people for eons.

Sonya's younger sister, Sheryl, frequently changes plans without letting Sonya know. Sonya has eaten alone more than once when she and Sheryl were supposed to go out to lunch—Sheryl gets busy with a project at home, works right through lunch, and doesn't call. Last weekend, Sonya and her husband got all dressed up, ready for a night out, and Sheryl was supposed to babysit. But at the last minute, Sheryl decided to go shopping instead, and Sonya and her husband stayed home.

Linda and Jim's dinner guests never return the invitation—Jim is just too difficult to be around. When Linda tries to tell a story, he interrupts her. He takes calls on his cell phone in front of everyone else, forcing you to listen to his conversations. If you offer to help Linda with the dishes, that's when Jim insists you need to learn all about his new stereo system, and when you try to say good-night so you can get your babysitter home on time—well, that's when Jim walks you around the house, explaining all the expensive remodeling plans he is making.

Linda has grown weary of Jim's self-centered behavior, but nothing she has said or done has influenced him to change. Poor Linda—unlike her dinner guests, she is faced with Jim's attitude all the time.

Evelyn is an alcoholic in denial. She lives alone but within driving distance of her son, Tony. She calls several times a day, and often at night, begging Tony to come and visit her. When she comes to Tony's house, she scares her grandchildren with her ravings. Tony and his wife, Jen, have had to call the police several times to find Evelyn after she ran out of the house crying over an imagined slight.

Tony has tried reasoning, being firm, and ignoring Evelyn, all to no avail. Tony's wife has tried to be supportive, but she has had it with the chaos Evelyn causes, and she blames Tony for not standing up to his mother.

Though their situations are very different, Sonya, Linda, and Tony have this in common: *Someone important to them is affecting their lives in very negative ways.* Can you relate? Then you're living with a difficult person.

Who's Pushing Your Buttons?

Most of the time, the difficult person pushing your buttons is someone you care about—your spouse, a parent, someone you're dating, or a co-worker, neighbor, or friend. There are all sorts of difficult people, and they can be found in many areas of your life:

- The controlling boss who micromanages people
- The dependent adult child who constantly drains you
- The detached husband who will not communicate
- The blaming wife who will not take responsibility for her part
- The victim who wants you to rescue her
- The irresponsible boyfriend who can't be depended on
- The self-absorbed mom who sees only her own needs
- The moody co-worker who controls the work environment
- The gossiping relative who forms divisions in the family
- The alcoholic or drug addict who causes chaos in the lives of others
- The "rageaholic" dad who has everyone walking on eggshells

The list could go on and on.

How Do You Feel?

Relationships are the delivery system for so many of the good things we need in life—love, safety, grace, warmth, encouragement, truth, forgiveness, and more. These elements make life meaningful, purposeful, and enjoyable. But life with a difficult person is none of those things. Instead, you probably experience a range of negative emotions and reactions.

OUT OF TOUCH

I cannot reach him is a common feeling. You want closeness, empathy, or intimacy, but it just does not happen. Maybe the other person doesn't respond to you and withdraws himself emotionally. Maybe his actions are not consistent with his words, so you feel confused. Or it may seem that your feelings don't matter to him and his choices. You may feel deeply isolated, alienated, and lonely.

OUT OF LOVE

Often, someone dealing with a difficult person feels love for that individual is waning. If the situation involves a spouse or a dating relationship, you may no longer feel that you are in love. You don't experience the warmth and affection you once did, or that you would like to. It is as if all the crazy things the difficult person is and does are destroying the affection you once had for him or her.

OUT OF OPTIONS

Another common reaction to difficult people is the feeling that you can't do anything to change the situation. You've probably tried reasoning, suggesting, and threatening, and nothing has made a difference. You have found no way to improve things, and you feel helpless, impotent, and frustrated.

OUT OF CONTROL

When you are with your difficult person, it is as if her issues trigger your darker self. You may find yourself angrier than you want to be, overwhelmed with sadness, or withdrawn. Sometimes you may feel revengeful or mean, playing payback in the relationship. God designed us so that good relationships draw out and encourage the best in us: love, care, and the ability to give freely of ourselves. If you don't like the person you are when you're around your difficult person, it is time to make some changes.

OUT OF PERSPECTIVES

Difficult people often seem to have power to make you lose perspective. You may find, for example, that you have become obsessed with a troublesome relationship. Have you ever had lunch with a friend, for example, when it seemed a third person was also there? You were so focused on a difficult person in your life that the troublemaker might as well have picked up the tab. Such obsession is a clear signal that the difficult person is running everything (and should be fired from that role!).

OUT OF HOPE

Perhaps the most serious effect of being with a difficult person is losing hope. You think that things will always be this bad and that you should either leave or resign yourself to this existence.

When hope is gone, we give up. Hope is what fuels us to strive for a better life and future. "Hope deferred makes the heart sick, but a longing fulfilled is a tree of life" (Proverbs 13:12).

My experience is that much of the time when hope is gone, it's because you do not possess the information, the resources, or the courage you need to create change. Either you haven't known what to do, didn't have the support to do it, or were too afraid to make effective changes.

Hope Can Be Reborn

If for any reason you are in a dangerous situation, you need to protect yourself. You may need to physically remove yourself from the situation for a while in order to safely deal with the problem.

But having said that, in my experience *most people give up too soon*. This book provides strategies that can turn things around. So for now, let's say that, with some exceptions, it's best to stay in your difficult relationship, but in a different way than you have been. This time, with the help of this book, you can face the issues, learn the skills, and get to work at making things better.

The nature of love is to stay. Love relationships (as opposed to task or business relationships) are designed to develop, grow, and mature over time as two individuals also grow. Love is about things getting better, not worse, the longer you stay in the relationship. It is worth the trouble to look at ways the love you had for your difficult person, and still want, can be reborn.

The fact that you're reading this book may mean you haven't decided to abandon your difficult relationship yet, although you may be on your last try. Or maybe you feel you can't leave. You may be in a job you really need. You may have circumstances in your marriage that prohibit your leaving. There may be a family member who will remain in your life no matter what. My prayer for you is that this book will change your *I have to get out of this relationship* or your *I can't get out of this* to *I don't want out of this.*

Change Is Possible

Difficult people can and do change, in deep and long-lasting ways, all the time. God has been in the business of changing difficult people for eons. The apostle Paul, who wrote much of the New Testament, said that before God transformed him, he himself had been "the worst of sinners" (1 Timothy 1:16).

There are no guarantees of change, as people always have freedom to choose poorly. But it is good to have the right and full perspective here: Your button-pusher can be outgunned. There is a lot you can do, and a lot that God can do through you: "I know that you can do all things; no plan of yours can be thwarted" (Job 42:2). We are talking about God himself on your side!

In my counseling, speaking, and personal life, I have seen changes and growth take place in so many ways:

- THE CONTROLLING BOSS BEGINS TO LIGHTEN UP AND GIVE PEOPLE SLACK.
- THE DEPENDENT ADULT CHILD GROWS UP AND ESTABLISHES A LIFE OF HIS OWN.
- THE DETACHED HUSBAND BEGINS TO OPEN UP EMOTIONALLY.
- THE BLAMING WIFE APOLOGIZES AND BECOMES CONCERNED ABOUT HER PART.
- THE VICTIM BECOMES STRONGER AND MORE AUTONOMOUS.
- THE IRRESPONSIBLE BOYFRIEND BECOMES MORE RELIABLE.

- THE SELF-ABSORBED MOM LEARNS TO BE CONCERNED ABOUT OTHERS' EXPERIENCES.
- THE GOSSIPING RELATIVE SETS LIMITS ON HER TONGUE.
- THE ALCOHOLIC OR DRUG ADDICT GETS HELP AND BEGINS TO CONTRIBUTE TO LIFE.
- THE "RAGEAHOLIC" DAD BECOMES KINDER AND LESS REACTIVE.

Life with a difficult person is like having a giant traffic jam in your connection, blocking all the good things you want in the relationship. But as the other person "gets it," begins to take ownership of his problems, and then begins to change, the jam gets unblocked and the traffic flow resumes, distributing all the good you are wanting.

When you've finished this book, you will understand difficult people like you never have before. You'll be able to stop dealing with your button-pusher in ways that don't work, and you will have a plan for utilizing seven different resources to help your difficult person want to change. Many people have learned how to help their button-pusher become an easier person to be around. You can too.

MAKING LIFE BETTER

1. Who is the difficult person in your life? Which of the reactions described in this chapter do you most identify with?

2. We are not talking about perfection here. You are looking for improvement—perhaps a lot of improvement—but not perfection. Do you have idealistic or perfectionistic leanings? Toss perfectionism out the window right now if you want success with your button-pusher.

CHAPTER 2
UNDERSTAND WHY PEOPLE ARE DIFFICULT

*Healthy individuals dedicate themselves
to bringing their sinful tendencies to the light of God and His people.*

Brian and Cindy have a son, Dylan, in his mid-twenties. Dylan didn't finish college, moved back home, hasn't kept a steady job, has a chronically ungrateful attitude, and shows indications of drug use.

Cindy, in particular, had a hard time with the fact that Dylan does not listen to them. "I just cannot believe it," she said, over and over. "We've given him everything. We've tried to reason with him and be supportive, but he acts like we're against him. Why won't he listen and grow up?"

So I said to Cindy, "Let me ask you a question. You're at the zoo, walking past the lion cage, and you notice the door is wide open and the lion is coming out. He sees you. What happens next?"

Cindy went along with it: "I guess he would eat me."

"Probably so. And why would he do that?"

"Because he was hungry?"

"Sure, and because that's what lions do. With Dylan, you keep expecting a lion to listen to reason and walk back into the cage."

You may be in Cindy's position, struggling to accept that someone you love is the way he is. Or you may simply be baffled and confused. Either way, you need understanding about why people are difficult people, so you can begin to create an environment for change.

A Character Problem

Behavior is a symptom of how a difficult person looks at life. Don't get sidetracked by behavior. The first thing to understand is a difficult person's *character*. As Jesus said, "Every good tree bears good fruit, but a bad tree bears bad fruit" (Matthew 7:17). So rather than dealing only with behavior—the fruit—we want to look at the tree itself: at character.

Elsewhere Dr. Henry Cloud and I have defined character as that set of abilities you need to meet the demands of life.[1] There are six basic aspects to character. They are the abilities to:

- SUSTAIN MEANINGFUL RELATIONSHIPS
- TAKE RESPONSIBILITY AND HAVE SELF-CONTROL IN YOUR LIFE
- LIVE IN THE REALITY OF YOUR AND OTHERS' IMPERFECTIONS
- WORK AND DO TASKS COMPETENTLY
- HAVE AN INTERNAL MORAL STRUCTURE
- HAVE A TRANSCENDENT SPIRITUAL LIFE

With these abilities, life goes pretty well. And the reverse is true: Many problems in life can be traced to deficits in these areas.

AN OWNERSHIP PROBLEM

We all have character issues. What sets difficult people apart is not adequately taking responsibility for, or *owning*, their part in their issues and how their character problems are affecting other people.

Most of us strive to grow and mature past our character issues. A difficult person, however, remains stuck in an immature state. Here are some of the things you may hear your difficult person say, either with words or with actions, that indicate an ownership problem.

I'M NOT THE PROBLEM

In one family, the children were tremendously injured by their mom with a venomous attitude, and all struggled emotionally and relationally as a result. As adults, they wanted a relationship with her and wanted their children to know their grandmother. They held an intervention, an intense meeting to try to get through to her. But she took it as a personal attack and shunned them for a long time.

The last I heard, she was living in a little apartment by herself, with very little help, because she had run everyone off. On her refrigerator was a piece of paper with the handwritten words "I'm not sorry." That is her life statement. And that symbolizes what I mean by a lack of ownership.

I CAN DO WHAT I WANT

Remember Cindy and Dylan? Cindy responds to normal confrontations and concerns. If someone tells her "This bothers me," she listens, evaluates, and tries to rectify the situation, reconcile the relationship, and become a better person.

A difficult person plays by different rules. Soul-searching, confrontation, feedback, and another person's hurt feelings don't motivate him to change. Instead, he rationalizes, denies, and minimizes the difficulty he causes, or he blames you.

I'M MORE IMPORTANT THAN YOU

Difficult people often see themselves as central. Their experience is always more important than yours. Sometimes they become angry. Sometimes they think they are being persecuted. They might be clueless about their effect on you. Often they have a diminished capacity for empathy for the feelings of others and perceive other people as nagging, blaming, persecutory, controlling, or—worst of all—insignificant.

I'M HAPPY THE WAY I AM

Often, difficult people been this way for a long time; therefore, they are comfortable with how they are. It feels safe. That's why one goal of this book is to show you how to help difficult people be less comfortable in their dysfunction, so they will *want* to change.

HOW DIFFICULT PEOPLE ARE HARDWIRED

So ownership is the problem, but *why* do difficult people fail to "own their stuff"? This also is important to understand, because it can help direct your approach to dealing with a button-pusher.

Here are some of the more important reasons difficult people don't take responsibility for their lives.

THEY MAY LACK KNOWLEDGE AND EXPERIENCE

Many difficult people have little awareness of emotional realities. They may have grown up in families that never talked about relationships, emotions, growth, and spirituality. Or they may have had a lot of chaos in their lives and turned away on the inside in order to manage life.

THEY MAY BE FEARFUL

Some difficult people resist hearing feedback about themselves because they are afraid of being seen as a bad person, or afraid that if you really know them you will leave. Still others have a deep fear of being overwhelmed and unable to cope.

I once counseled a man whose coldness had ruined a couple of marriages, alienated his kids, and caused big business problems. On the surface, he seemed not to care. But in counseling as he started feeling safer, he began to experience his need for relationship. He also realized a deep terror—he was afraid he would be so vulnerable to others that people would be able to really hurt him. [2]

THEY MAY FEEL ENTITLED

These individuals believe, secretly or overtly, that they are special and above others; therefore, they should not be subjected to the same rules others are. Often, the entitled person is self-absorbed and grandiose, with little awareness of the feelings of others. The grandiosity comes from no one ever lovingly popping the balloon of selfishness to help him see that others are as important as he is.

THEY MAY BE ENVIOUS

Envy is not desire. Desire can be a very good thing, for it drives us to get what we need—jobs, relationships, opportunities, and the like. And when a desire is fulfilled, we experience peace and contentment.

The opposite is true with an envious person. When he gets the promotion, the money, or the relationship, it is not enough. Something else now becomes the reason for his unhappiness. The problem is always outside himself—his unsupportive wife, his demanding boss, the church that doesn't meet his needs.

THEY MAY BE STUCK EMOTIONALLY

Some difficult people have an emotional or psychological disorder that renders them less able to see what they are doing. Some acute depressions, for example, make it difficult for a person to see beyond her pain to the effect she has on others. Anxiety, panic, and addictive processes can also distort thinking. This does not mean the person *wants* to continue whatever she is doing. But she *is* stuck in pain that is clouding her thinking and functioning.

THEY MAY BE SPIRITUALLY BLIND

We all have tendencies to go our own way, away from God's care and His path. That is the essence of sin. Healthy individuals dedicate themselves to bringing their sinful tendencies to the light of God and his people. But others have a shallow view of their sin, or do not see it at all, or have given themselves over to the control of sin. Spiritual blindness causes a person to miss seeing what is inside that needs to be healed by grace and the power of God.

THEY MAY HAVE PSYCHIATRIC OR MEDICAL ISSUES

Medical or psychiatric conditions can distort perceptions of reality. For example, thought disorders, psychotic processes, and hallucinations can wreak havoc on a person's ability to be aware of his issues. It is always good to consult with a psychiatrist if you suspect there is evidence of this kind of disorder.

THEY MAY BE AFFECTED BY THE DEMONIC

There is a real devil, whose agenda is to separate people from God. "Be self-controlled and alert. Your enemy the devil prowls around like a roaring lion looking for someone to devour" (1 Peter 5:8).

Not every problem has a demon under a rock. But some do. If you suspect this sort of force at work, find people in your spiritual community who have experience in these matters *and who also believe in the power of emotional, psychological, and medical issues*—the Bible teaches a balance of factors.

Reality Is Larger Than We Are

Here is what is critical for you to believe as you begin to understand your difficult person: His lack of ownership should create problems *for him.* This is not being mean; it is just true, and it means hope for you and for him.

Reality is larger than we are. We can't fight long against gravity, magnetism, or nuclear force. It's the same with relationships. We reap what we sow (see Galatians 6:7), in the good or bad consequences of our lives. So character deficits and resistance to taking responsibility should cause life not to work well for your difficult person. That can be a great incentive for change.

MAKING LIFE BETTER

1. As you develop your plan for dealing with your difficult person, you want to be strict on the issues, but warm toward the person. That's how all of us want to be treated, and that is what works best. One way to help you do that is to keep his good qualities in mind. Make a list of those now.

2. Think about ways you might be enabling or rescuing your difficult person from experiencing the consequences of his actions. Maybe you're always there for him, or threaten without following through, or encourage without confronting. It is worthwhile—and one of the things we will discuss later—to analyze if you might be part of the problem.

Chapter 3
Diagnose the Disease

We are responsible, but we cannot transform ourselves.

Now it's time to move from difficult people in general to your particular situation. Use this chapter to help you realistically and carefully "diagnose the disease," so to speak. This exercise will involve time and energy, and taking such a close and personal look may be harder than it seems. Don't rush the process. In fact, it is probably best to do this in stages and use the time in between to reflect. Here are the things to look at.

Symptoms: Focus on the Fruit

To begin, determine what behavior or attitudes of your difficult person are affecting your life and the relationship itself. In chapter 2 we called behavior the *fruit* in someone's life. Here are some examples.

- MY BOYFRIEND DRINKS TOO MUCH.

- MY HUSBAND IS WITHDRAWN AND DISTANT.

- NOTHING I DO IS GOOD ENOUGH FOR MY BOSS.

- MY HUSBAND IS PUTTING US IN FINANCIAL JEOPARDY.

- MY DAD SCARES ME WITH HIS TEMPER.

- MY TEENAGED DAUGHTER IS OUT OF CONTROL.

- MY WIFE SPENDS TOO MUCH.

- MY HUSBAND IS INTO INTERNET PORN.

- I CAN'T DEPEND ON MY FRIEND TO BE RELIABLE AND
  RESPONSIBLE.

- MY ADULT CHILD WON'T GET A JOB AND LEAVE HOME.

It is important to clearly state what is going on. "He can be such a jerk" or "She's impossible" aren't helpful in focusing on the real issues. Try to determine the biggest single problem. A "rageaholic" who doesn't pick up his socks, for example, should have to deal first with his anger rather than his sloppiness.

EVALUATE SYMPTOMS

How severe is the problem? This is important for you to evaluate, as it will help determine your course of action later on.

For example, in the case of an anger problem, the level could be:

Not very severe. Perhaps the person scares you with his temper, but only a few times a year.

Moderately severe. The person may have frequent fits of rage, creating family chaos.

Extremely severe and urgent. There may be physical violence or someone could be in danger. (You may need to be prepared to take quick action—calling someone for help, finding a shelter, or even calling the police.)

CAUSES: FOCUS ON THE ROOT

This requires a little more digging. As we discussed earlier, behavior is generally a fruit of deeper matters. Focus on the *root* now, not the fruit. Let's look again at our list of problems, and this time, let's examine the possible causes or influences. I have listed two for each problem. Both could be present, and there are many other possible causes as well.

If you find that you are overwhelmed or confused by the complexity of your difficult person, seek out a counselor and tell her what you know, asking for clarification. This can be very illuminating and help you focus on what is really going on.

- My boyfriend drinks too much.
  He hasn't become an adult yet.
  He is medicating internal pain.

- My husband is withdrawn and distant.

  He is unable to open up emotionally.

  He is self-absorbed.

- Nothing I do is good enough for my boss.

  He is critical.

  He is isolated from relationship in his life.

- My husband is putting us in financial jeopardy.

  He is impulsive and has little self-control.

  He lacks empathy for the distress he causes.

- My dad scares me with his temper.

  He intimidates when he needs to admit he is wrong.

  He avoids feeling helpless when he can't control someone.

- My teenage daughter is out of control.

  She doesn't have, or refuses, structure and authority.

  She is disconnected and isolated.

- My wife spends too much money.

  She is immature.

  She is meeting some need in a symbolic way.

- My husband is into Internet porn.

  He retreats to fantasy to avoid some negative reality.

  He feels helpless and powerless around his wife.

- I can't depend on my friend to be reliable and responsible.

  She relies on good intentions rather than faithfulness.

  She overcommits herself.

- My adult child won't get a job and leave home.

  He feels no concern for taking care of his own life.

  He does not possess the skills to enter life.

PROBE SEVERITY

You need to understand how deep the character issues go. For example, is the emotional distance of your husband so profound that he speaks to no one in his life about anything but news and sports? Or can he talk about personal issues at some level but not deeply? Or does he open up with others but not with you?

Here's another example. Does your adult child feel entitled to your caretaking and never make any move to become independent of you? Or does she move out and fail and move back in, hating it all the time?

Does your critical boss incessantly find fault for large and small, real and perceived offenses, unaware of what she is doing? Or does she sometimes offer praise, but mostly criticism? Or does she encourage others but come hard down on you?

TEMPERATURE: THE OWNERSHIP PROBLEM

Evaluate ownership. Is the problem *minimal*—the person responds to an empathic but clear confrontation? Is it more *serious*—the person sees what she does but excuses it, rationalizes it, or minimizes it? Or is the ownership problem *severe*—the person is unaware of what she does, or she blames her behavior on you or on others?

Sometimes people weave in and out of denial. When they feel safe and loved, they admit to difficult behavior, but when they are afraid or threatened, they deny it. Some people admit to problematic behavior but simply aren't aware or do not care about its effect on others.

COMPLICATIONS: CAN'T VERSUS WON'T

This is another important aspect to look at as you figure out what is going on with your difficult person. Is she unable (can't), resistant (won't), or some combination of both?

Look at the level of concern the person has over the problem behavior. Is his life marked by a general sense of care for others and responsibility for himself? That argues for inability. Or does he show a lack of empathy and a failure to take ownership of what he does? That speaks for resistance.

There also is a more covert but fairly common form of this problem—resistance disguised as inability, or a won't *posing* as a can't.

In group counseling, Amy often criticized of other people and then laughed and said, "Just kidding." Whenever others in the group confronted her on it, she collapsed into tears and said, "I didn't mean it; it's my past coming to haunt me." So I said to her one night, "Amy, I'm sorry, but while I do believe you're a sensitive person, I just don't think you're as fragile as you appear, nor as sorry as you appear. It seems that you are using this issue to be able to be angry at people without having to experience their anger at what *you* do. That's not fair, and it's not good for you or for them."

Amy was very upset at my statement and wanted to leave. But the group supported her and at the same time affirmed my belief that she was more resistant than unable. To her credit, Amy was able to see that she was afraid to be direct with others.

The point is, go for what you and other safe people *see*, not just what your button-pusher *says*. Doing shows more than saying. Pay attention to covert signals.

The clear but tough message of the Bible is this: *We are responsible, but we cannot transform ourselves.* This forces us to look outside our own strength to God and his answers.

Just because your addicted adult child is responsible for his drug use doesn't mean he has the power or ability to become clean and sober. Just because your husband is responsible for his use of Internet porn doesn't mean he has the capacity to stop. There are strong and dark forces moving in all of us, including believers in Christ, and we all need grace, love, support, truth, wisdom, and time to mature into changed people.

That is why it is important that you be well into the process of doing your own growth work, as we will discuss in the next chapter, in order to effectively take the next steps toward helping your difficult person change and grow.

MAKING LIFE BETTER

1. Plan now when and where you will set aside time to consider the situation you face with a difficult person as described in this chapter.

2. If you do not already know a professional counselor whom you trust, ask friends, co-workers, or your pastor for a recommendation. It is good to have this name as a backup as you go through the process described in this chapter.

CHAPTER 4

RELEASE WHAT DOESN'T WORK

Reality is always your friend.

Karen wanted help dealing with her dad. He was mean and belittling to her mom. He criticized Karen unmercifully when they talked. He became combative at social gatherings and embarrassed her, and when things didn't go his way he got quiet and sulked for days.

When I asked Karen, "How much are you contributing to the problem?" she was surprised and upset. "*My* part? What are you talking about? I'm the one who's subjected to verbal abuse. I'm the one who has to call him to make up. I'm the one who has to put Mom back together after he hurts her feelings."

I said, "Karen, your dad is a very difficult man, but there are things you are doing that help to keep him sick and mean, and you can do something about them. They are *your* baggage, and I would be glad to take a look at them with you if you would like."

To the extent you avoid owning your part in the problem, you will continue in the problem. Your contribution, like Karen's, may be much less weighty than your button-pusher's. That does not let you off the hook. Jesus had a pretty direct statement about this: "You hypocrite, first take the plank out of your own eye, and then you will see clearly to remove the speck from your brother's eye" (Matthew 7:5).

Let's take a look at some of the unsuccessful things we do with button-pushers, why we do them, and how we can stop doing them. It's time to let them go.

DENYING

You may find that you minimize your button-pusher's hurtful, annoying, or selfish actions. You may say to yourself or others, "He has so many good qualities" or "He's just having a bad day. Denial keeps our head in the sand, wishing and hoping that things aren't as bad as they really are.

We deny for the same reasons button-pushers do: fear of loss of love; not wanting to appear or be bad; avoidance of conflict, guilt, or pride, for example. But denial can rob you of life and years. Reality is always your friend.

Remember Cindy, who denied the severity of Dylan's condition? She was protecting herself against the sadness that the son she loved was not a good person, at least at that point in his life. But when she accepted it, then she was able to truly help Dylan in effective, meaningful ways.

Spiritualizing

To *spiritualize* is to distort true spirituality. There are three ways to spiritualize with a difficult person.

The first is *preaching*, trying to motivate the difficult person by telling him Bible verses or principles. It is sometimes wiser, instead of preaching the Word, to *actually live the Word*: become the most loving, fun, responsible, honest person you can be.

A second way to spiritualize is to become *passive*, doing nothing to solve the problem and simply praying and hoping instead. But we are co-laborers with God, and He often shows us things to do in addition to prayer.

The most destructive spiritualization is *superiority*, feeling so close to God and unable to relate to the button-pusher because he does not understand the spiritual truths that we do. This is a dangerous perch to rest on. It is rooted in pride and is not truly spiritual at all.

Reasoning and Reminding

Probably the most common error is to believe that the solution you need is all about reason and logic, a meeting of the minds. You think that if the difficult person truly understands that what you are asking for is a good thing, he will comply and change.

But disagreeing with him is often a button-pusher's signal to tune you out. He is not thinking *Hmmm, she's got a good point. I never thought about that.* Instead, what he hears is like the old cartoon about what a dog hears when you scold him: *Blah blah blah Spot blah blah blah blah Spot blah blah blah.*

A close cousin to the reasoning approach is reminding (we call it nagging too). Nagging assumes that the person just needs to be reminded to do the right thing. When you nag, you are perceived as controlling and authoritarian, so the button-pusher reverts to a childish state and rebels against the "parent" by increasing the bad behavior. I see this in a lot of marriages and dating relationships. The love, trust, and passion deteriorate quickly when two adults become a kid and a parent.

REACTING AND BLASTING

Let's all confess together now: *I let my difficult person push me to say stuff I wish I'd never said.* As we saw in chapter 1, a button-pusher can influence you to be someone you don't want to be.

This capacity to react and blast away is due to some dependency we have. That is, we are looking for something from our difficult person, perhaps warmth, affirmation, or love. Then, when it is not forthcoming, we respond in desperation and high emotion. More often than not, the button-pusher thinks, *See? I'm not the problem; you are the crazy, raving person.*

BACKING OFF

This is the opposite of reacting and blasting. There is a polite, hopeful part in all of us that is somewhat conflict avoidant. So you wait politely until the button-pusher sees the errors of his ways and comes to you to help him change.

It can be a long wait. Often the last thing the difficult person wants to do is ask for help. The more silence there is, the more assent he perceives and assumes. I once worked with a woman who thought that her impulsive, "spendaholic" husband would notice her silence and withdrawal and ask what was wrong. They were almost bankrupt before I convinced her that her plan was not working.

SPLITTING GRACE AND TRUTH

Grace is, as the classical theologians have defined it, unmerited favor. Truth, on the other hand, is about what is, what is real. Grace and truth need each other.

Truth operates to protect grace and love in the same way that your skeletal frame protects your heart. These must be in tandem: Grace gives us the fuel to live, grow, and change; truth protects and structures the process.

Bob and Katie had a teenage daughter, Sarah. Sarah's grades had been dropping dramatically; plus, she was hanging with the wrong crowd, lying to her parents, and sneaking out at night.

Katie's response was to try to encourage Sarah. "When she makes a mistake, I hear her out and try to listen to what her experience is like. I want her to know that she is loved and safe." Sarah knew that her mother would not give her consequences and would be sympathetic. Nothing really changed except that Sarah liked her mom.

Bob's response was discipline and consequences. "I don't even listen to the excuses anymore. I tell her the expectations and what will happen if she doesn't follow up. We need for her to see that she has to get her act together." Sarah is afraid of her dad and avoids him.

Katie had grace, Bob had truth. Each approach was polarized against the other. The problem comes in when you split, rather than integrate, grace and truth.[1] Like Bob and Katie, you become ineffective when you don't have enough of each.

FEELING RESPONSIBLE

There is no question that we should all scrutinize our lives and actions to see if we are doing what we should. But we also need to investigate whether there's a pattern for taking on too much responsibility for the problem.

Taking too much responsibility for the problem also happens when we put ourselves in charge of the difficult person's choices and the outcome. This is often due to some lack of personal definition and separateness.

Enabling

Enabling happens in any number of ways. You may avoid confronting your difficult person. You may provide comfort, warmth, and support for him even when he is being destructive. You might cover for him with friends and family or pay his rent when he refuses to work. When he is unkind, you might blame yourself for provoking him.

Love and enabling are not the same thing. Love can be loving and still have zero tolerance toward irresponsibility, selfishness, and manipulation. If you are enabling your button-pusher, you may think you are caring, but in effect you are hating him. There is some pain that he may need to experience in order for the lights to go on.

Threatening without Follow-Up

Just don't ever do this. Don't. When you deliver empty or inconsistent threats, *you are training your difficult person to ignore you.* You are saying, "I'm going to blow off steam now. If you will sit tight and wait it out, you can go back to doing whatever you were doing, and nothing will happen to you."

A man once told me about his girlfriend who had blown up at him for his inappropriate flirting, "It's okay; she's all bark and no bite." He was even a little proud that he had figured her out so well. He was dead on. And he did not feel any need to change his hurtfulness!

So if you bark, be prepared to bite. If you aren't, get yourself a muzzle!

Giving Up Too Soon

This is the "one time should do it" approach, the hope and expectation that one appeal—or one confrontation or invitation or threat or consequence—should be enough.

Sometimes I hear "I've tried everything and nothing seems to work." Often, however, what this really means is that you have tried some of the *ineffective* things in this chapter, which are doomed to fail. Chapters 6-12 present seven different resources to help you create a change environment for your difficult person. You may find that you are using some of these resources already, but all seven are essential.

Before you can utilize the seven resources, however, use the next chapter to decide what success will look like.

MAKING LIFE BETTER

1. A good antidote to denial is to go to a safe and truthful friend who knows your situation.[2] Ask if you are avoiding the seriousness of your difficult person's situation.

2. If you lean more toward either grace or truth, there is a reason. Talk with a friend or counselor to discover what it might be, so that you can begin to show both grace and truth to your difficult person.

Chapter 5

Decide What You Want

When circumstances are the stormiest,
clarity of vision has kept many a sojourner steady on the path.

When I counsel people about a difficult relationship, I often ask what their vision is for the future of the relationship. Many times, the answer is a quizzical look, as if I'm speaking Martian, followed by something like "What are you talking about? I just want to survive and not go crazy."

It is understandable that those in a difficult relationship have trouble with the concept of vision. The word has to do with positive things in life like high goals, dreams, and shared aspirations. Large companies often began with a dream. Churches and ministries have the same origins. Humble beginnings but lofty goals—that's the nature of vision. Those with a button-pusher are too busy playing defense, warding off the effects of the relationship, worrying, and sometimes "just trying to survive." It's hard to have a vision in the middle of a nightmare.

You Need a Vision

At the same time, however, you do need a vision. This goes far beyond mere survival. The remaining chapters of this book provide seven different resources for you to embrace and use. You will need to do things that you haven't done before or are afraid of, or that are unpleasant for you, yet are the necessary things that will bring about change. And *vision* will help you sustain the effort and courage required.

This is especially important in difficult relationships, as there is generally some resistance, or even escalation, in the other person when you begin to make the important changes that must occur. You need a place inside yourself to keep you on track.

Let's briefly describe *vision* as "the mental picture of a desired outcome that gives you heart and focus." It is an image you craft and construct in your mind that encapsulates whatever goal you have. Its purpose is to carry you through the dark times so that you can see them through to achieve the goal. People who want to lose weight might put a photo of a bathing suit that they want to get into on the refrigerator. Those saving for a home might have a diagram of the dream house on the wall. An individual working for a job promotion may have a desk plate with his name and the position engraved on it.

Vision is given by God and is modeled by Him. One of Jesus' final statements on the cross was "It is finished" (John 19:30). The "it" was His vision to redeem the world to himself by enduring death for us, and He completed His mission. That is the nature of vision. When circumstances are the stormiest, clarity of vision has kept many a sojourner steady on the path.

This chapter will help you create a particular, specific, and individual vision, tailored to your situation with your difficult person.

ASPECTS OF VISION

How do you go about creating a vision for what you want to see? Here are some key components to consider.

PRESENCE OF THE GOOD VERSUS ABSENCE OF THE BAD

This is a hard one. It's difficult to see beyond a desire for a husband to stop yelling and throwing things, or for a wife to lay off the constant nagging. These involve the cessation of bad things, which is certainly important, but that's not enough. If all that happens is that a bad behavior ends, you are probably selling yourself short. Far better to want him to be approachable and able to deal with conflict lovingly, and for her to be patient and vulnerable when there is a problem.

RELATIONSHIP

Relationship is the greatest part of life. You are most likely in a personal relationship with your button-pusher. Paint into your vision the relational components that you would like from your button-pusher, such as closeness, safety, intimacy, respect, freedom, trust, and mutuality. These are important.

THE BOTTOM LINE

As you are developing your vision, never forget what we discussed in chapter 2: Most of the time, the problem of all problems in a button-pusher is that he does not own, or take responsibility for, the issues that affect his life and those around him.

Your vision must include the picture of this person being open to being wrong, to being sorry, to hearing how he affects you, to seeing himself as a contributor to the problem, and to entering a process of change if needed. When this place is reached, and it may not come right away, everything speeds up and goes better.

WHAT WILL YOU SETTLE FOR?

Your vision also needs some sort of minimum requirement. That is, you will need to clearly articulate the smallest sort of change you will accept as being a good thing. A husband who doesn't withdraw and sulk for weeks, but who won't get into a growth group to look at his issues, is still better for you than one who hasn't changed at all. A wife who overspends a lot less than she did, but still overspends, is an improvement. An alcoholic who stops drinking from willpower alone is no longer a danger to himself or others for now, though he runs a relapse risk and often manifests irritability or depression that the drinking has been masking.

By no means am I saying that you are to be satisfied with external restraint that involves no internal shifts of attitude, feeling, perspective, and value. That can—and should—be a lifelong desire and goal. At the same time, however, stay away from chronic criticism. You don't want your button-pusher living under your not-enough mantra. He will ultimately rebel against it, and you both lose. A better stance is "This is good, and I want even better for us."

AIM HIGH

You may be discouraged, but still aim high in your vision. As the old saying goes, aim at a star and you may hit a stump; aim at a stump and you may hit nothing at all.

The highest vision is that your difficult person will be transformed from the inside out. That vision involves much more than changed behavior; it involves a changed heart. And it integrates the external behaviors, troublesome though they be, with the internal world, which is a more thorough and complete process. Here are some examples of high aims for your difficult individual.

- THE IRRESPONSIBLE WIFE WHO IS FINANCIALLY RUINING THE FAMILY MATURES AND BECOMES DEPENDABLE AND RELIABLE.
- THE SELF-CENTERED FRIEND WHO WILL NOT PAY ATTENTION TO YOUR FEELINGS AND CONCERNS DEVELOPS THE ABILITY TO PUT OTHERS BEFORE HIMSELF AND HAVE GENUINE AND DEEP EMPATHY.
- THE MOODY ADULT CHILD WHOSE OUTBURSTS CAUSE CHAOS BECOMES STABLE, KIND, AND FUN TO BE AROUND.
- THE CONTROLLING BOSS DEMONSTRATES GRACE AND FREEDOM TO HIS SUBORDINATES.
- THE HEAVY-DRINKING HUSBAND NOT ONLY STOPS DRINKING BUT WILL RESOLVE THE EMOTIONAL PAIN INSIDE THAT MAKES IT DIFFICULT TO BE AROUND HIM.

ALL THINGS ARE POSSIBLE

You may very well be thinking, *This is not reality and it is not possible.* I agree that when it comes to human freedom, there are few guarantees. But there *are* two guarantees that are important to know. One is that all things are possible with God (Matthew 19:26); and the second is that God is on your side, and He has designed your button-pusher to be better off and happier when he is doing life God's way. So put skepticism on the back burner for now, and work on crafting your vision.

MAKING LIFE BETTER

1. Write out your vision for your relationship with your difficult person. Remember to include the key components and to aim high.

2. Think about two people you know who have a good relationship. What are some of the good things they are able to do together? For example, they may spend time together, travel, minister to others, or participate together in hobbies, the arts, or sports. What good things like this would you like to experience in your relationship with your difficult person? Include these details in your vision.

CHAPTER 6
INVITE GOD IN

God does not want to be your Prozac. He wants you.

So far you have worked to understand why difficult people are the way they are and what the real problem is with your button-pusher. You have learned what doesn't work, and you've formed a vision for your relationship in the future. Now you're ready to put seven different resources to work to help you create an environment for change with your difficult person.

This chapter is about the first resource, God. If there is anything in the world that will get a person thinking about God, it is a difficult relationship. It can put you straight down on your knees.

GOD GETS IT

You care about a button-pusher and want things to go well between the two of you, yet that person is free to choose his attitudes, his behavior, and whether he even wants to be in the relationship with you. God understands this situation. He knows it conceptually, and He knows it in experience. God lives in it every day, caring about us and wanting a relationship with us that is for our best, yet He gives us the freedom to say no to Him, and we often do.

Jesus' words illustrate the depth of His emotion and empathy toward us: "O Jerusalem, Jerusalem, you who kill the prophets and stone those sent to you, how often I have longed to gather your children together, as a hen gathers her chicks under her wings, but you were not willing" (Matthew 23:37, 38).

HE GETS YOUR BUTTON-PUSHER

Difficult people can be complicated people who create complicated relationships. Yet God shines the light of truth and understanding on these matters. He is the one who "knows the secrets of the heart" (Psalm 44:21). He is aware of the inconsistencies, the sudden mood shifts, the counterattacks and blaming, and all the things in your difficult person that mystify you. These are not mysteries to Him; rather, He can point the way through the mazes.

This is why inviting God in as your first resource for dealing with your button-pusher is not about being "religious." When you encounter a problem in everyday life—something you have little experience with—you call an expert or consult someone with experience. Literally, God has more experience dealing with difficult people than anyone.

It is also important to realize that God is "for" your difficult person, just as He is "for" you. God is an inexhaustible reservoir of grace and love, not only in order to help you to hang in there, but also for the difficult person. I have often prayed, "God, I am out of love for this person; sorry about that. Please give me some of Yours, because there's no more in here." And He does.

God takes clearly defined positions on many issues, such as deception (Psalm 101:7), lack of love (Matthew 24:12), selfishness (James 3:16), and irresponsibility (Proverbs 20:4). But as Creator, Father, and Redeemer, He loves and wants good things for your button-pusher.

HE GETS THE PROBLEM

God is the architect of relationships. He designed the nature of human connections, in all its complexity, and how the connections work. He is relationship itself.

In His role as architect, God mapped out life and relationships according to certain rules and laws that operate in certain ways. As He does not fail, neither do His laws. When we live in submission to them, life tends to work better. When we are antagonistic to them, things should—and do—break down.

Take the law of sowing and reaping, derived from Galatians 6:7: "Do not be deceived: God cannot be mocked. A man reaps what he sows." The basic idea is every action has a consequence. If we sow love, humility, and responsibility, we should reap those. If we fail to sow these good things, we should experience disconnection, reactions to our pride, and losses.[1]

I have seen the law of sowing and reaping work in powerful ways when people allow their button-pusher to experience it. Conversely, I have seen it interrupted by well-meaning rescuers and enablers. "The Lord disciplines those he loves" (Hebrews 12:6). Do not make the mistake of getting between your difficult person and God's rules.

HE GETS THE PLAN

God has an intent and plan for your button-pusher, just as He does for you. That intent is reconciliation. Reconciliation is the process whereby estranged parties resolve their differences and become allied again. It is one of the things that God is most interested in for humanity: "God was reconciling the world to himself in Christ, not counting men's sins against them. And he has committed to us the message of reconciliation" (2 Corinthians 5:19).

God wants your difficult person to be reconciled to his own heart, to others, and to God himself. The behaviors of difficult people generally indicate that at least one of those three areas of reconciliation is not operational. The person may not be fully connected to God and his life. He is certainly not reconciled with you and probably not with others. And he likely has parts of himself that are not reconciled with other parts, which puts him in conflict, especially in relationships. One of the best things you can do is to ask God to reconcile your difficult person in these three areas of life and relationship.

God Wants You

God is not very interested in solving your relationship problem simply to make you happy. Happiness is a byproduct of being connected to *Him*. God does not want to be your Prozac. He wants *you*. "If anyone hears my voice and opens the door, I will come in and eat with him, and he with me" (Revelation 3:20). In and through your difficult relationship, God may be working with you to get to know Him better.

I have a friend whose husband is a former button-pusher. The struggles she went through in her marriage changed her in profound and permanent ways. For example, her view of pain is now one of embracing it. She does not enjoy pain, but she does not turn from any pain that might cause her to grow spiritually and personally. She sees God behind it, and moves toward it.

What Faith Looks Like

Abraham followed God in faith, as you will have to do: "By faith Abraham, when called to go to a place he would later receive as his inheritance, obeyed and went, even though he did not know where he was going. By faith he made his home in the promised land like a stranger in a foreign country; he lived in tents, as did Isaac and Jacob, who were heirs with him of the same promise. For he was looking forward to the city with foundations, whose architect and builder is God" (Hebrews 11:8-10).

God Calls

Abraham was called. God extends himself to us in many different ways. Faith is about recognizing the call—in the form of a burning bush, a Bible verse that jumps off the page, a conversation on the phone, or an e-mail from a friend.

Pay attention; listen for the call. Attending is not easy in a world of pagers, cell phones, and instant messaging. You will probably need to find some structured minutes in your day to listen for the still, small voice amid the din of modern life.

Confess to God that you are at the end of your resources with your difficult person. Ask Him for help, and let Him know that you are open to any way He responds and any direction He says. Make it truly "Thy will, not my will" (see Matthew 26:39). This only makes sense, as your solutions have not helped you. It is truly time to listen to God's voice.

WE HEAR AND RESPOND

Abraham went to a place he didn't know. He chose to go in faith, without attempting to control the situation. He landed in unfamiliar territory, in a foreign land, out of his comfort zone.

You might think, *I am not in a comfort zone either*, but that is not true. You may be miserable in your relationship, but there is comfort in the known bad—you may know how to manage by walking on eggshells. You may have figured out how to protect the finances from his irresponsibility. You may know to avoid him when he's having a bad day. These things work in a survival mode sort of way, and there is comfort in these structures.

I can pretty much assure you that growing in faith will take you out of your comfort zone with your button-pusher. You may have to say things you are afraid to say, or do things you aren't used to doing. You may have to deal with some things inside yourself that are painful. But when you look at it realistically, what are the alternatives? They are reduced to returning to your old approaches, which haven't worked, or giving up, which means things might even get worse.

FAITH MEANS HOPE

Abraham had a future hope. He lived in tents, but he looked forward to a city with foundations. "Foundations" refers to stability and strength. It is the hope of a future with peace and security.

You will be living in a tent for a while—the tent of new experiences, thoughts, feelings, and risks. But there is a city waiting that you can look forward to, the city of a better life: the life of God, a life of relationship and freedom and a life that may see your difficult person enter the process of growth and change himself. That is worth a camping trip in a tent!

Understand that this life of faith is not about desiring or wishing. That puts the power in the hands of the wisher, you. The power of true faith is rooted in the substance and reality of the object of that faith, God. No one can deal with difficult people better than He can. I have seen God do miracles with button-pushers over the past many years. God's presence and His process of growth *can* be trusted. Invite Him in.

MAKING LIFE BETTER

1. You may already be praying something like "God, help me know how to handle my person." Now add to that prayer "Help me see what You want me to learn from all this *about my life with You*."

2. Ask God to place you in the right position to be part of the growth process for your button-pusher. Whatever He asks you to do, it will be for you, the other person, and your relationship.

CHAPTER 7

GET READY TO GROW

There is something to be said about your life being so full
that empty people desire what you have.

I'll never forget the day I accidentally discovered the mystery behind Kevin and Cheryl's disconnect. Kevin came in late for their counseling appointment, and it wasn't the first time. Cheryl blew up. Then out of the corner of my eye, I noticed that Kevin was smiling, a small and secretive smile.

At first he tried to deny it, but Cheryl had seen it too. Finally Kevin admitted it. He was invested in looking like the normal guy with the crazy wife.

"I understand your anger now," I told Cheryl. "Kevin does set you up sometimes. But you will never have the marriage you want until you stop being so easily provoked by his covert actions. From now on, I want you to say, 'I feel disconnected and hurt. Was that on purpose, or did I do something to make you mad? Would you tell me what it was, so we can reconnect?'"

Cheryl making the first move of health began to get to Kevin. Eventually, the covert button-pusher changed in some substantial ways. Your own personal growth is your second resource for dealing with your difficult person.

BE A CHANGE AGENT

Remember that difficult people lack ownership of their problems. Until that is addressed, nothing significant happens. One way you can be an agent for change is to be a person of high ownership yourself. As you take proper responsibility for your life, you shift the nature of the relationship toward growth. As you own what you need to and don't own what is not yours, your button-pusher has less room to blame and deny and more incentive to change.

This can be explained as a matter of light and darkness. The more your life is in the light—that is, exposed fully to love, truth, and the growth process—the more you become light. The darkness and the hiding of the difficult person react to that light. He cannot stay neutral for long, as light and dark are not compatible. He may be drawn to the light and begin to change, becoming a person of light himself. Or he senses that many things might have to change, so he becomes antagonistic toward the light and moves against it or away from it. "The light shines in the darkness, but the darkness has not understood it" (John 1:5). Either way, there is movement, and that is good.

Reclaim Your Happiness

One of the most powerful principles to help you begin to see change in your relationship with a difficult person involves reclaiming control over your own happiness. The Bible says that your life is *your* life, and you will be called to account for how you live it. "So then, each of us will give an account of himself to God" (Romans 14:12).

Own Your Life

Amanda had a conflict with her best friend, Pam, and Pam abruptly ended the relationship. Several months later, Amanda's pain and emotions were still quite strong. She couldn't get her friend out of her mind. Since Pam had given no explanation for the rift, Amanda was left with no closure, which made her feel guilty and confused. She even got somewhat obsessive about the problem, leaving messages and e-mails for Pam and talking to mutual friends about what happened. Pam was in control of Amanda's happiness and well-being.

Amanda had a legitimate complaint, in that she needed an answer from Pam to be able to make sense of things and let it go. But she also needed to let it go even with the loose ends. To be able to move on, Amanda made the lack of closure another aspect of her grief: She missed Pam, and she missed having answers and information. Amanda was able to stop her obsessive behaviors and retrieve her life through grief and letting go.

Get involved in whatever was good and meaningful before the problem with your button-pusher began. Plug into people who will empathize but who also let you know they want a more robust relationship with you than just problem-solving. Do some things that have nothing to do with your difficult person. Own your life.

DEPEND ON THE RIGHT PEOPLE

You desire good things from your difficult person: love, respect, tenderness, responsibility, affirmation, and the like. There's nothing wrong with wanting something. Desire holds people together and helps them meet each other's needs. But it is a different matter to put a major aspect of your life on hold, waiting for the other person to cooperate so that your life will be better.

For example, if you have a difficult co-worker, you may find yourself thinking about the problem all the time. You talk to friends and other co-workers about the issue. You make many different attempts to change things. But you find that each time the difficult co-worker acts out again, your own day is shot. The button-pusher is in charge of your happiness! You feel frustrated and powerless, and the difficult person does not change.

The solution is to end your dependency upon the button-pusher and place it instead with people who can fulfill your needs for affirmation, empathy, structure, and reality. When you do that, there are often two very important results.

First, the difficult person begins to miss you, as you are not clinging and intruding on him. There has to be space for the other person to feel longing. Second, when you are not dependent on him, the button-pusher is more likely to experience his own issues and emptiness. When you say, "I'm going to be with some friends; see you," he is less able to avoid his own darkness and to experience whatever it is he needs to deal with.

FACE YOUR FEARS

It can be easier to live on the defensive with a button-pusher than to face the anxieties of becoming a separate and independent person. It is like the parable Jesus taught about the workers who received five talents, two talents, and one talent to invest. The one with the least hid his talent in the ground because he was afraid. Not surprisingly, the master was unhappy with him and called him wicked and lazy (Matthew 25:14-30).

Get some time and space to discover what your talents, passions, and interests are. You may find that you must deal with fears of failure, or fear of new scenarios, or fear of change itself. Face the fears and become a new person. Be in charge of your life, instead of waiting for a difficult person to change before you have a life. As you take back control of your life, you are not being mean or unloving to your button-pusher. In fact, you are doing something very good for him. You are being transformed into someone who can deal with his issue lovingly and not out of fear, need, or desperation.

Become What You Are Requesting

When you begin to grow and change, you become an example of how love, relationship, responsibility, and freedom all work together for a good result. There is something to be said about your life being so full that empty people desire what you have.

Here are two practical ideas to help apply your life and growth to your button-pusher's.

Put Down the One-Up Role

Avoid any semblance of one-upmanship, as if you are above your button-pusher because you are happy and independent, or as if you are happy because he is not doing well and you are. That is a dangerous and arrogant position. Remember that you are also unfinished in some way, needing the grace and help of God and others.

Define Who You Are

One of the most powerful aspects of your life that can help your button-pusher is becoming a *defined* person. That is, you need to become clear, honest, and direct about *who you are*, *what you think*, and *what you want*.

A defined person isn't easily thrown off balance. He is like an anchor in a storm. He cares, but he does not change who he is. With a difficult person, he keeps an even keel. For example, he is kind toward clinginess, yet he keeps some distance and separateness. He is strict about rage and either doesn't tolerate it or leaves until it is over; he doesn't try to fix it.

This sort of definition provides a structure for a difficult person to interact with, experience, learn from, and internalize. Often, difficult people are very unstable inside and need someone who is strong to give them the structure they need.

There is a huge difference between desiring someone's growth and *depending* on someone's growth. As the saying goes, pray like it all depends on God, and work like it all depends on you. Though you must hope in God and His process, yet, as we have said, people are free, and you have no *guarantee* that your changed life will change your button-pusher. Work out in your head the possibility that your difficult person may not get the message. Though you may be saddened, it will be from a place of love and comfort. Keep on investing in life and good things, stay full of love and support, and you will be a beacon of hope to your difficult person.

MAKING LIFE BETTER

1. To what extent are you owning your life? Ask yourself if you are willing to grow and change.

2. What do you most fear about reclaiming your happiness from your button-pusher? How will you begin to overcome that fear?

Chapter 8
Find Others Who Are Safe and Sane

You are guaranteed failure with a difficult person
if you do not surround yourself with the right people.

I counseled a woman whose brother frequently was argumentative, provocative, or critical. She was a very isolated person with severe trust issues, and with no one to support her, she could not deal effectively with her brother. We went to work helping her learn to establish healthy connections with other people. Eventually she got plugged in to some good relationships. And when that happened, things began changing with her brother.

She was able to confront him when he got out of line. She was more direct about how she wanted to be treated. She even had more empathy for his struggles. He became more aware of his actions, and their relationship became more mutually beneficial.

You are guaranteed failure with a difficult person if you do not surround yourself with the right people, *because it takes relationship to transform relationship*. Safe and sane people are your third resource for dealing with difficult people.[1]

There are two ways good people play a role as a resource for you. The first has to do with your own life and growth. The second is about providing specific help for your situation with a difficult person. There is often overlap between the two. The important thing is that *all* the functions and processes listed below must be going on, whether it is with two different groups of folks, or one group, or some combination of the two.

You Need People for Life and Growth

Relationships provide valuable supports for all of us, whether we are dealing with a difficult person or not. These supports are like your computer's operating system, the foundation that makes everything run.

Acceptance

Acceptance is part of the provision of grace that we all need. To be accepted is to be cared about in your current condition, whatever it is, just as you are: "Accept one another, then, just as Christ accepted you, in order to bring praise to God" (Romans 15:7). You need people in your life who don't require you to have it all together in order to be connected and safe.

UNDERSTANDING

You need people who can "be there" with you. It helps that someone truly "gets" your experience: "The purposes of a man's heart are deep waters, but a man of understanding draws them out" (Proverbs 20:5).

FEEDBACK

We often have blind spots that can only be noted by others. Ask for help to grow as a person, and don't resist any authentic feedback. Do others see emotions in your facial expression that you aren't experiencing? Do they note some negative attitude you should come to terms with? Are there ways of perceiving yourself or others that should be addressed?

People in a group context can be an especially rich source of good feedback. Like a second family, the group can provide what your first family did not, and can help repair whatever damage the first one may have caused.

You Need People Who Can Help

In addition to people who can provide the supports listed above, you also need other things from people willing to help you navigate your situation with a button-pusher. Here is what to look for.

NORMALIZATION

Normalization is the ability to convey a sense that you are not aberrant, different, or bad for having a button-pusher. You may be contributing to the problem in some way, but you are not causing the button-pusher to behave as she does. Your life *is* difficult, and that's the way things are.

WISDOM

Defined as the capacity to live skillfully, wisdom provides the path you need. People with wisdom can direct, guide, correct, and provide insight for you about your situation.

Some people have wisdom from the school of experience; they have dealt with difficult people in their own lives. They can give you deeper understanding of your relationship and warn you about pitfalls to avoid.

Good pastors, counselors, and therapists have wisdom that comes from formal training; they have studied button-pushers and know what makes them tick and what helps them change.

EXPERIENCE

Sane people who are on your team can help you get experience you may need. For example, they can role-play with you what you need to say to your button-pusher. They can critique and suggest better ways to do it. Role-playing is the dress rehearsal that prepares you for the real thing, which we will talk about in chapter 10.

Recently at a conference, I initiated a role-playing exercise and asked for a volunteer to play a defensive, blaming button-pusher. I played the role of someone handling the situation well. I then asked those at the conference what their reactions were.

One said, "I never knew it was okay to keep getting back on track." Another said, "I thought being loving meant letting the other person control the talk." Others said things like "I have never seen how to put grace with the truth. I always get mad or give in. I don't think I'll be as rattled next time." Role-playing with people in your support system gives you experience and confidence.

REALITY AND PERSPECTIVE

Most people who care about a difficult person feel pretty uncertain and disoriented about their own opinions, thoughts, and experiences. Safe and sane people can reorient you to what is real.

I often prescribe to people with a difficult relationship that they create a "relationship sandwich." Before they have a confrontational conversation with the button-pusher (we will go into more detail on this in chapter 10), they meet with their supportive group and get prayer, encouragement, advice, and love. Soon after the difficult conversation, sometimes just a few hours later, they meet with their supportive group again to process what happened: "You said the right thing. . . . I would tell you if I thought she was right about what she said about you, but I listened to your story, and I think she blamed you for everything. . . . I am proud of you. What a giant step! . . . Hey, you may think she hates you, but we love you. . . . Keep up the good work."

HOLDING THE LINE

In chapter 11 we will deal with setting and keeping limits with your button-pusher. Safe and sane people serve as guardians of these limits when you are in danger of not following through. This is a beautiful example of how the body of Christ, the Church, is supposed to support the weak member: "Carry each other's burdens, and in this way you will fulfill the law of Christ" (Galatians 6:2).

I saw this in action with a woman whose husband was having an affair and had left the home. She was turned upside down by the situation, but quickly got connected in a growth group I was leading.

One day she came to group and told us her husband had called and was planning to come over. She missed him terribly, even after what he had done, and wanted to see him. She knew she was likely to have sex with him. She had given in several times before.

The group heard her out, then talked to her about the realities of what she wanted and what giving in would do to her and her plans. I could see her gathering strength as people talked to her. Finally, she said she was going to cancel the visit, and she did. In time, her husband gave up the affair, got help, and eventually returned home. The group gave her strength to hold a line when she was not able to keep it for herself.

DIRECT DEALINGS

There are times when other people can help by being directly involved with the button-pusher. Generally speaking, the more the difficult person respects or identifies with these other people, the more powerful the effects.

Meeting and talking. When you are too weak to manage the button-pusher alone, other people can meet with him and talk to him. This has the effect of driving home the reality that there is a problem.

Interventions. An intervention is an intense meeting with a person who is in denial and out of control in some area, such as substance abuse. People who matter to that person, such as his family, friends, and co-workers, gather and confront him lovingly but directly about what he is doing to himself and others and urge him to get help. There are people around the country who are formally trained in conducting interventions for various problems.

Neutralizing. I once consulted with a professional and his boss about their relationship. The man thought his boss was controlling, and the boss thought his employee couldn't handle authority. After listening, I told the man I sided with the boss. "He hasn't asked anything of you that isn't within the purview of the job. Sounds like you are resisting having a boss."

The man thought about it and said, "You know, that makes sense."

The boss was irritated. "That's exactly what I've been saying! How come you can hear it from him?"

"I don't know," said the man. "He just says it in a better way."

I didn't say it any better than the boss. But not being the boss, I was perceived as neutral.

Pressure over time. Your safe relationships can perform a very valuable service by keeping up their presence in the button-pusher's life. In a caring way, they keep the pressure on. They commit to waiting him out, in a sense. They continue calling, meeting, processing the problem with him, and inviting him to change. They offer their help and support.

This sort of pressure can help melt resistance and secretiveness.

Character patterns tend to get worse in darkness and improve in the light of relationships.

How to Plug In

Get plugged in yesterday; do not go it alone! "I can do this myself" is either pride or fear talking, and they are no good for you. There are different places to find people who can be part of your supportive network.

"Starbucks Relationships"

These are friends you meet with when you can to catch up with each other. They can help a lot and provide support and encouragement, allowing you to come away from the informal meeting with courage to face another day.

Structured Support

The severity of your situation with a difficult person will let you know whether you need more than friendship connections. I generally recommend going to the next step, which is some sort of small group that meets regularly for general spiritual or emotional growth. The structure provides stability and reliability of contact, and that is very important. Growth groups and some Bible studies are good resources here.

THERAPIST-LED GROUPS

A more focused help is a group that deals specifically with your type of difficult relationship. This may involve people who are having the same experience, and is led by a trained facilitator or therapist. Here, there is more time and energy spent on you and how to address your situation.

ONE ON ONE

Individual help can be very beneficial too. At this level, the time is dedicated to your situation and ways to resolve it. Even if your difficult person is a spouse or adult child who will not go to counseling with you, go alone for your own growth and support, and the benefits will flow over to your button-pusher.

MAKING LIFE BETTER

1. Who are the people in your supportive network? List them and also list which of the processes described in this chapter they can offer. What kind of help do you need to add to your support system?

2. Take the risk, get on the phone, and call the churches in your area to learn what group growth opportunities they offer.

CHAPTER 9
TAKE A STANCE

God is "for" us. This is the stance of grace at its essence.

Scott was at the end of his rope with his daughter, Kim. Nothing was working. He thought he needed a better plan.

I said, "That's probably true, but you aren't ready yet for a plan. You haven't figured out your basic stance toward Kim as a person. You're all over the map. Before we talk about a plan, you need to take a stance with Kim that won't change, and then after that we can start planning."

What is a stance? Simply put, it's a point of view toward someone. It is a broad, guiding attitude that helps direct you. Taking a stance is your fourth resource for dealing with a difficult person.

Here are four stances, all related, that you need.

I Want What Is Best

The first stance to take is to be "for" the other person and your relationship; you want the best for her and for the two of you together. Nothing could be more counterintuitive than this, but it is the best stance to take. God is "for" us. This is the stance of grace at its essence—that just as God favors us, we are to favor others.

Why is this stance so important? Change and growth are never easy, even for people who embrace it as a good thing. Your button-pusher has avoided that path for many years. No one can successfully execute real change without the grace and support of others to help them along the way. It is just too hard. You are asking your button-pusher to repent, see things your way, listen to feedback, be open to getting help, and a host of other things. She will need the warmth, time, and patience that grace and love bring.

What "For" Does Not Mean

First, being for someone doesn't mean you agree with what they are doing. Grace is like the ocean, surrounding us and constantly supporting us. Agreement is a specific and finite boat on that ocean. If you don't agree, you change boats to another position, but you stay on the ocean.

Here is a tip: Be careful not to allow your button-pusher to assume that grace and love equal agreement. Clarify, clarify, clarify. "I want to make sure this is straight between us, Denise: I totally support, accept, and love you; I am for you, and for us as a relationship. But at the same time, your moodiness with the family is a real problem, and I am going to keep working on dealing with it."

Grace and being for someone also doesn't mean rescue. When we rescue, we take the weight of problem onto our shoulders rather than keeping it on the shoulders of the difficult person. Being "for" never means removing someone from reality. Rather, it means giving someone the love and support required to bear and deal with reality.

Being for someone is not about what's fair. At times, it doesn't seem fair to be supportive of the button-pusher in any way. We have done so much, and she has done so little in response. But God was for us when we least deserved it. He came to us when we had walked away from Him. Realize that you need grace also. When you are truly honest about who you are, you see more clearly how much it means that God is for *you*, and what a plight you would be in if that were not the case. Those who appreciate that God is on their side can more freely give that grace to others.

My Growth Is Good for Us

Related to the "for" stance, but somewhat different, is the stance that your own path of growth will benefit the life of your difficult person. The things you are learning and the changes you are making, as we discussed in chapter 7, should help your button-pusher. Your growth can be a blessing to him. You should be becoming the most encouraging, loving, fun, humble, honest, responsible, cool person that your button-pusher has ever seen! He should be saying to himself, *Wow, I've got a good deal here!*

What you don't want is to begin to feel superior to your button-pusher because you are growing and he is not. If you are growing, your heart and empathic abilities are also.

I Care about Freedom

Even though your difficult person uses his freedom to cause problems for you, you still must adopt a stance of preserving his freedom to make bad choices. He needs to be free to be in denial, selfish, withdrawn, irresponsible, or controlling for there to be any hope that he will make an authentic choice to turn around. (This does not mean that your support for your button-pusher's freedom should permit him to hurt you. Take responsibility to protect and guard yourself if he is unsafe with you.)

Let your button-pusher know: "I want things to change between us, and I need for you to change some things. But you don't have to. You can choose not to. I will not stop you. I may have a response, and we can discuss that. I may also protect myself. But I want you to know that you have freedom, and I will not try to control you. If you change, I want it to be because you think it is best."

You simply cannot lose with this stance.

I Am Willing to Confront

This stance has to do with the attitude that the relationship is important enough to you that you will endure conflict and disharmony in order to attempt to make things better.

Steve was an intimidating fellow who controlled Ann and their kids by blowing up and being angry when he didn't get his way. Ann was the peacekeeper who tried to tiptoe on eggshells around him so he wouldn't get upset. She calmed him down when he had his tantrums by complying with what he wanted. But the next time he was crossed, he blew up again.

I showed Proverbs 19:19 to Ann: "A hot-tempered man must pay the penalty; if you rescue him, you will have to do it again." I told her, "You're taking responsibility for Steve's temper, and it's getting worse, not better, over time. Something must change. I want you to take a stance for Steve, yourself, and the marriage, and I think the stance should be that you are willing to confront him."

Ann wasn't excited, but she agreed. She did a lot of work to adopt this stance. She dealt with her fears of people's anger. She got support. She role-played conflict resolution. And she began to confront Steve, first in my office, and later at home alone with him.

Steve didn't like any of this, but he stuck with the counseling and with Ann. Later, after all this had resolved, Steve was grateful to Ann. He told her, "I would probably still be running everyone in my life away if you hadn't been willing to not back down."

MAKING LIFE BETTER

1. Which of the four stances described in this chapter comes easiest for you? Which one is most difficult?

2. What legitimate needs does your button-pusher have? What does he like to do? What makes him feel loved? How you can help him in his own goals? Certainly don't be party to any wrong or harmful actions, but as much as possible, move toward his life.

.

Chapter 10

Use Words Well

It wouldn't be a problem to you if it didn't affect you in some negative way.

Even with the resources we've presented so far, if you aren't also talking to your button-pusher about the problem, he might take that as a sign that you are happy with the way things are. This chapter unpacks the elements of using words well, which is your fifth resource for handling difficult people.

Every conversation has two dimensions: tone and content. Tone has to do with how your voice sounds, and content is what you say.

Tone: Talking from Your Heart

The tone you begin and conduct the conversation with must serve the purpose of conveying the first stance that we discussed in chapter 9: You are "for" the difficult person and the relationship.

BE WARM

Warmth conveys safety and care, and that stands the best chance of keeping your button-pusher from becoming even more wary or defensive than she already is.

You may not feel warmth for her because of what she has done to you. If so, confess and process those feelings with your support system before you have the talk. Otherwise you risk escalating things and not getting the results you desire.

SPEAK FROM YOUR EXPERIENCE

Talk from the heart. Use "I" statements as much as possible, staying with what *you* feel, think, and perceive. Don't sound as if your reality is the final authority. Read these two statements to spot the contrast, and plan to pattern what you want to say after the second example, not the first.

> *"You are angry with me all the time, and you need to stop."*
>
> *"It seems to me that you are angry with me pretty often, and it is difficult for me to be close to you."*

CONTENT: A CONVERSATIONAL GAME PLAN

Now let's construct a game plan for what you want to say to your button-pusher. The following elements are in a general order, but there can be some flexibility. You will know each next step by the response you get.

AFFIRM THE GOOD

Begin by affirming what is good in the other person and in your relationship. You might start something like this:

> *Thanks for meeting with me. I wouldn't have asked you to take the time unless I thought it was important, and I want you to know that you are important to me. I am on your side, and I want things to be good for you and for us. There are a lot of great things between us that I want to keep and develop. You have so many good points, like your work ethic and your sense of humor.*
>
> *All I want to do in this conversation is to talk about a problem in order for us to solve it. I want to get it out of the way because it comes between us, and it hurts me. I want to get on with a good life and closeness with you. Does that make sense?*

Wait for a response, and then if you need to, clarify: "I'm saying that I love you and I want to be close to you again, and this problem is like a boulder in the middle of the road. I just want the boulder out of the way, because I want you. Does that make sense?"

Hearing out your button-pusher at the beginning of the conversation will help him hear you later. So don't go into the entire problem yet; just touch on it to give him context. Say something like this:

I want to talk to you about our relationship, especially my experience of you as being too angry with me. But first I really want to understand what it's like for you—if you see this the same way, or if I'm doing something that isn't helping.

Now wait. Your button-pusher should feel the grace and permission you are extending and present his side of things. Do not make the mistake of correcting his perception of you here. That does not further your mission; in fact, it can lose ground for you. Be still and understand his opinion. You are not agreeing; you are listening.

However, don't hear him out forever. Some button-pushers won't have the structure to stop. So, when you think you have the basics, say something like this:

Okay, I think I get your end of it: You do get angry and withdrawn sometimes, because the job is hard, but you think that I am overreacting and it's not as bad as I say. And I make things worse when I nag and don't get off your back. Do I have the main idea of it?

If he has some valid points about your contribution to the problem, agree, apologize, and let him know you will change. Say something like this: "I think you are right, that I nag and don't let go of things with you. I can see how that makes matters worse. I'm sorry, and I will work on that."

STATE THE PROBLEM

Now, directly and simply, state what it the problem is and how it affects you and others. Talk in terms of what can be seen, observed, even measured. Mention specific behaviors that illustrate the problem: "You get overly angry at home. You yelled at me last night when I asked why you were late to dinner."

STATE THE PROBLEM'S EFFECT

It wouldn't be a problem to you if it didn't affect you in some negative way. Now tell the button-pusher how the problem affects you and your relationship. The more you show how what he does hurts the "we," the better your chances of breaking through his resistance. Here's an example:

> Your yelling scares me, and the kids too. They woke up last night. And I really distance from you when you do it. It just shuts me down inside, and I can't get past it, even though I want to. I miss being close to you, but it is impossible when you are that mad. Then, when you aren't angry anymore and want to be close, I stay away from you because my feelings haven't changed.

You are trying here to elicit empathy and compassion from him regarding how his behavior is hurting people he loves and relationships he values. If, however, he is too self-absorbed, afraid, or uncaring to be moved, you may have to say something like this: "So you admit you get irrationally angry and scared and distance me and the kids. But you also seem to be saying that you don't care. Are you saying that?" Sometimes, having to own a statement like that will help a button-pusher begin to see what he is doing.

OWN YOUR STUFF

There may be more that you need to own that the other person has not mentioned. If he has not brought those issues up, but you know they exist, take initiative to talk about them:

I know that I have made things worse for you and us. I have done a lot of threatening without following up. I can see how I confused things by saying one thing and doing another. So I want you to know that I am aware of this. I am sorry, and I want to stop.

REQUEST CHANGE

Next, say what you want to see change. Keep it uncomplicated. You want him to stop doing a negative thing, or to start doing a good thing that he is neglecting. Here are some examples:

- "I want you to stop being so angry with me."
- "If you are angry, let me know what is wrong in a calm way so we can talk about it."
- "If you are really mad at me, go take a walk or call someone before you bring it to me, so that you are calmer about it."
- "I want you to talk to me about your anger and admit that you are angry before you start blaming me and yelling. That way we can deal with your anger together."

Pay attention ahead of time to the possibility that what you desire may be something that is beyond the button-pusher's ability to change. A substance abuser may not be able to stop. A depressed person cannot simply to choose to be happy. If this is the case, request something that will help empower the other person to change. Tell the substance abuser you want him to get into treatment now. Tell the depressed person you want him to call a therapist this week. Using the example of the angry husband, if he has a history of sincerely trying but failing to control his anger, tell him you want him to talk to a counselor or a pastor this week.

Deal with Deflection

Be prepared for resistance. The difficult person may deny, minimize, rationalize, or blame the problem on you. This is a signal that you have a second problem to deal with besides the issue you are bringing up. Stay in the game. There are approaches you can use to help get through his deflections of your message.

LISTEN, THEN GET BACK ON TRACK

Hear out the excuse or blame, but then refocus on your request for change: "I understand that you think you wouldn't be angry if it weren't for me. And I'd like to talk about that sometime soon. But I want to get back to my request for you to not be so angry at me when you get home." This is being in control of yourself and your part of the conversation. During the hearing and owning parts of the talk, you already did listen, consider, own, and apologize for whatever you have done.

SHIFT THE FOCUS TO THE RESISTANCE

If, after several attempts to refocus on the problem, the other person won't admit what he is doing, turn to making his resistance the problem. This can be very helpful for both of you, and it probably lies at the core of the biggest issue of the relationship anyway. Say something like this:

I'm feeling pretty helpless right now. Every time I attempt to show you that your anger is a problem for me, you either blame me, tell me

I'm overreacting, make excuses for it, or get angrier. This isn't being productive for either of us. I'm becoming aware that I can't talk about problems with you in a way that solves them for us. So a lot of our issues don't ever get resolved. I can't imagine that this is pleasant for you either. Can we work on this as a problem?

Another tactic is to transfer responsibility for receiving feedback on him. Say this:

When I confront you or give you feedback, it doesn't go well. You feel like I am being unfair, or don't understand you. I don't want you to feel that way, because I'm not those things. Here is what I would like: I want you to tell me how to tell you the truth in a way that you can feel okay about hearing it.

LEARN TO WARN

The Bible teaches that if several people go to a person with a problem, and he doesn't listen to them, then they are to move to consequences and limits (Matthew 18:15-17; 1 Corinthians 5:1-5). We will deal more thoroughly with limits and consequences in chapter 11. But before you set limits, you need to warn the other person that they may be coming.

TIMING

It is probably best not to go into warning until you have tried a few times to work it out by talking. You also may want to bring in people from your support system, as we discussed in chapter 8. However, if all else is failing, warn of the coming result. You might say:

> You aren't admitting that your anger is a real and serious problem. I am not going to keep talking to you about this. But I want to let you know that I am not going to tolerate it either, even if you do insist that you aren't doing it. The next time you raise your voice at me in an angry manner, I will leave the house and go to Nicole's for a while. And if you continue, I will take further actions until you have taken steps to stop.

When you are warning, be firm, strong, and direct. If you don't think you can follow through, don't say it. Work first on being strengthened through your safe and sane relationships, and then warn when you are prepared.

Remember that God has been warning us, and telling us to warn each other, for ages (Ezekiel 3:33). It is a gift and a blessing to give someone a warning to change. It may be what begins to turn life around for your button-pushing relationship. But if the response is not what you would desire, then it is time for the actions prescribed in the next chapter.

MAKING LIFE BETTER

1. Plan the conversation you need to have. Write out the steps outlined in this chapter; then write what you might say that pertains to your situation.

2. Role-play the conversation with a good friend, a counselor, or another of your support people.

CHAPTER 11
ACT WITH CONFIDENCE

You have power in your relationship that you may not be aware of.

Tom had repeatedly asked his mother, Andrea, to stop calling his teenaged son, Matt, and saying negative and untrue things about Tom. He warned her that she was jeopardizing her relationship with all of them if she did not stop. It was time to go beyond words to actions. Tom told his mother that the family would not have any contact with her until she apologized and asked for forgiveness. Andrea kept calling, but Tom, his wife, and Matt would say, "If this isn't about apologizing, I'm going to hang up now." This happened several times, and then Andrea wrote them a letter saying she was cutting off all contact with them.

Two years passed. Then Tom got a call from Andrea. When he picked up the phone, she said, "I'm sorry for what I did. Will you forgive me?"

Sometimes it takes actions to give weight to your words. Your actions are your sixth resource for handling difficult people.

The Power of Actions

There are two actions you can take: first boundaries, and then consequences. A limit, or boundary, defines who you are and who you are not; for example: "I am for us both having freedom in this relationship, and I am against one of us controlling the other." It can define what is your responsibility and what is not: "I care about you, but I am not responsible for your emotions." It can define what you will tolerate and what you will not: "I will agree to some overtime each week, but I won't put up with your working so much that you neglect the kids."

If a boundary is ignored, then, as we saw in chapter 10, a warning conveys that if this continues, something will happen that will be unpleasant to the person violating the limit. Consequences enforce boundaries. A consequence can be either the presence of something undesirable to the difficult person or the absence of something desirable.

Find Appropriate Consequences

Andrea's consequence was losing contact with Tom and his family. The consequence was not *harmful* to Andrea, even though it brought pain. Instead, it had the dual purpose of protecting the family from her divisiveness and helping her realize that her attitudes and behavior were associated with results. Here are some principles for effective consequences.

NATURAL REALITY

First, when consequences mirror real life, the button-pusher is more likely to accept that he himself is the cause of his discomfort.

In the work world, for example, a person who is irresponsible with assignments and deadlines should naturally lose promotions, experience discipline and confrontation, and perhaps even lose his job. The closer to natural the consequences may be, the more you are out of the way and are less likely to be the object of blame.

THE RELATIONAL ASPECT

Consequences are also productive when they are about loss of relationship. We were designed by God to be relational creatures. So when an attachment is jeopardized, it tends to get our attention.

A man I know was in love with a woman he had been dating for some time. He was ready to be exclusive with her, but she didn't want to stop dating two other men she was also attached to. As time passed, she was unwilling to take responsibility for her problem and look at why she wanted to continue dating all three men. So my friend finally told her, "I'm moving on. I love you, but I can't stay in limbo. Don't call me unless you are ready to see only me." He was guarding his own heart and life.

The woman called several times to stay in touch, but my friend stood by the consequence and wouldn't talk to her. Finally, the deprivation caused her to miss him so much that it clarified for her that she would rather be without the other two men than without him. Ultimately they were married. The power of the loss of relationship cannot be overestimated.

MATCH THE SEVERITY

When you set a consequence, do not underreact or overreact. The "time" should match the "crime."

If your problem with a button-pusher is not very severe, set a minor consequence. For example, if a husband repeatedly won't listen to his wife when she wants to talk and watches TV instead, his wife might let him know that she may need to take a walk when it's time to help the kids with homework.

More severe circumstances, however, need more severe consequences. If a mate has an affair and is not repentant, a structured separation may convey the importance and hurt of what she has done.

LEVERAGE YOUR POWER

You have power in your relationship that you may not be aware of, because your button-pusher needs you, something you have, or something you provide. Otherwise, with the conflicts you have, why is she still in the relationship?

This is not about getting back at your button-pusher; it's about getting his attention so that he draws a connection between his behavior and his discomfort and makes the necessary changes. For example, a chronically critical person needs someone to listen and hear what she is saying. A consequence based on that need is to refuse to be present whenever she is being critical.

Here is a partial list of things you might possess and provide that your button-pusher, though he may not admit it, may genuinely need and want:

- COOKING, CLEANING, ORGANIZING, OR DOING CHORES
- FIXING THINGS AROUND THE HOUSE
- MAKING THE HOME A PLEASANT ENVIRONMENT
- HELP IN PROVIDING FRIENDSHIPS AND SOCIAL ACTIVITIES
- FINANCIAL RESOURCES
- A SOCIAL SETTING THAT MATTERS TO HIM
- FAMILY TIES, WHICH GIVE A SENSE OF BELONGING
- ACCEPTANCE OF HIS FAULTS
- WARMTH TOWARD HER
- EMOTIONAL PRESENCE WITH HIM
- PHYSICAL PRESENCE
- STRUCTURE TO HELP ORGANIZE HIM
- PLANNING TO GIVE FOCUS TO HER FUTURE

So you may at some point say something like this:

If you don't stop doing X, you will lose some benefits of being with me. I will be withholding them to keep myself safe, because I don't feel close or loved by you, and because I hope you will get the message that I am serious about your behavior and will not tolerate it.

WITHHOLDING SEX AS A CONSEQUENCE?

The issue of withholding sex must be thought through carefully and with others who are spiritually mature. First Corinthians 7:4-5 teaches that husbands and wives are not to deprive each other of sexual relations, to protect both spouses from temptation. This is an important biblical principle.

However, it's important to understand any passage in the context of the entire counsel of Scripture. For example, a husband is responsible to have a deep and self-sacrificing love for his wife (Ephesians 5:25, 33). If a wife is being pressured to have relations when her husband has a pattern of being indifferent to his wife's feelings or if she is mistreated by her husband, a consequence of refusing to have relations until this pattern changes may be appropriate. This is acting on the reality of how sexuality and relationship interact: The emotional union was designed by God to lead to the sexual union, not the reverse.

Follow Through

There is no substitute for following through on a consequence. This is when you walk your talk.

STAY CONNECTED TO OTHERS

Remember that your button-pusher is not the only one with dependencies. The more you need things from the button-pusher, the less likely you will be able to follow through. Get your needs met through your support system. Get involved with a church that is into process and supporting people in trouble. Make sure that your safe and sane relationships are on call for you when you want to cave in and forget the consequence.

NORMALIZE ESCALATION

Do not be surprised if your difficult person *escalates*, or increases, the problem behavior initially. If an angry button-pusher escalates and becomes violent or abusive, you must protect yourself and bring in more resources. But if it is safe to stay with your limit, the escalation often begins to subside over time.

KNOW WHEN TO TIGHTEN UP

Most of the time, the button-pusher will not begin to change the first time you establish the consequence. But don't be rigidly locked into one approach. Keep tweaking until you find the best combination.

A man who was running his family's finances into the ground blew off the warnings of his wife and friends. His wife's first consequence was to withdraw from him emotionally and to spend time away from him. Then she asked him to go to a support group, which he did. But after a period of time, his financial habits weren't changing. His wife finally asked him to move out until he began to be more financially responsible.

This mattered to him. The isolation, loneliness, and lack of warmth were quite distressing to him. For some time, he blamed her for being unloving, but eventually he agreed to submit his finances to others in their church who could help him.

KNOW WHEN TO LOOSEN UP

How do you determine when it is time to release the consequence? Here are some tips:

> *When change goes along with words.* You must insist that the person actually do things differently: start being more responsible, stop the criticism, end the drinking.

When change is sustained. This doesn't mean there won't be slip-ups and regressions. But a period of sustained change will indicate that the person is truly doing things differently.

When there is evidence of heart change. When a person is sorry about the pain he has caused you and others, that is good news. Look for true and authentic remorse and contrition.

When he gets into the growth process for himself. Give a lot of credence to your difficult person's intentions if he gets into some structure for spiritual and personal growth, such as a group or therapy.

When people you trust are okay with it. Your safe and sane relationships may see green lights you are missing or red lights you don't see. Get their perspective.

When God speaks to you. Stay attuned to the Holy Spirit and constantly ask God for guidance and direction. He knows your button-pusher's heart better than anyone.

MAKING LIFE BETTER

1. Natural consequences don't fit every situation. For example, a drug addict risks losing his health and dying from his substance abuse. One possible good consequence might be loss of support from important friends and family until he agrees to go to rehab. Which type of consequence is best for the situation you have with a difficult person?

2. Look up and read Deuteronomy 30:2-3. Can you think about boundaries and consequences with your difficult person in the same way? Boundaries and consequences are not punishment; they are love.

CHAPTER 12
COMMIT TO THE PROCESS

Continue doing all of the things today that could
make a difference tomorrow.

Time alone does not heal or change a person. Time all by itself actually works for the button-pusher's ends. If you do nothing and simply wait for her to change, she can wait you out, experiencing no discomfort.

But the right kind of time—which is time *plus* growth and action—can be very productive. So take an active approach to time. This is your seventh resource: your commitment to a process going on with your relationship over time.

BE PATIENT AND PERSISTENT

An approach to a person with low ownership over his behavior should never be looked at as a one-time event, but as a process. Many intentional events combine over time to create an environment that promotes change.

You must hang in there. You may have to repeat your conversations. You might have to restate boundaries. You are almost guaranteed to experience more than one trial of establishing and following through on consequences. Patience and persistence aren't very glamorous, but very few worthwhile things in life happen without them.

Deal with the Victim-Persecutor Dynamic

What causes your button-pusher to scream victim? If it is that you have disagreed with him, confronted, said no, or set a limit, that is suspect. For him, grace and getting his way equal love, and truth and confrontation equal hate.

If you see this in the process, do not ignore it. It is a character issue and must be addressed. Focus on the button-pusher's resistance as the problem, as we described in chapter 10.

Know What to Do When You See Results

Let your button-pusher know how much you appreciate his effort. Show him that whatever it is he values in your relationship is now more forthcoming because he is making good moves and choices.

I counseled a couple whose marriage was struggling, largely because the husband was very defensive and unwilling to admit faults and weaknesses. One day he said to her, "I think I've been screwing up with the way I have been treating you." His wife said, "Yes, you have been. But it really helps for you to say that. Thanks." She didn't come all the way back to him emotionally, but you could tell the temperature between them had warmed up.

Accept Gradual Shifts as Well as Breakthroughs

Most of the time, breakthroughs are the visible result of a great deal of invisible growth that has been going on through the steady application of the right resources. But sometimes you can see the small and gradual changes too: An irresponsible adult child is thankful instead of demanding. A moody friend asks for help. A spiritualizing person admits that she struggles in some area.

Sometimes behavior patterns change even before the button-pusher admits he has been out of control. It is very important to know this, so that if you see gradual behavioral shifts without confession or admission you won't be disappointed. Often the confession follows as the person continues to grow and becomes humble enough to face the truth.

Whether you see breakthrough or gradual changes, change is good. Recognize the shifts in your difficult person and work with your support team on what seems to be working and why. Keep the program going.

THE HEALING POWER OF GRIEF

There is always a possibility that your difficult person may not make any changes over time. That can certainly be a serious loss for you. Be willing to face your sadness and lost dreams. Grief is a process God designed to be the pain that heals, the process that makes us available for new, good things.[1]

I have a friend whose wife is a very difficult person. She is quite unhappy and negative and sort of infects other people with the disease. The two of them have been married a long time. My friend has faithfully loved her, though it has not been easy. And he has used the resources we've discussed in this book to promote change, sometimes a lot, sometimes not very much.

But if you were to ask him about his life, I am certain this man would say, "I have a good life." He does not feel that she has robbed his life of happiness. He has worked a lot on the ability to detach from her hurtful parts so that he doesn't get very wounded by her anymore. He enjoys the good times they do have. He has a deep faith, is involved in his church, and helps the less fortunate. He has good friends and many interests. He has grieved and let go of what he can't have from his wife, but he also lets himself hope that there still might be change.

RELATIONSHIPS REVISITED

When an infant is born, the first thing she sees is her mother's smiling face. The baby drinks in the safety and warmth she feels. When two people marry, they look forward to those times in which they can sit quietly together, needing no words, well attuned to each other's presence. And in the last moments of our lives, all of us desire to be surrounded by the people who have mattered most to us, holding our hand and conveying their endearments as they usher us into the hands of God.

God's design is that your difficult relationship would grow and transform into one that provides you mutual love and care. All the resources that you bring to bear upon the relationship do have great power and potential, for they are given by God, who desires that all of us return to Him and grow into His image.

Your button-pusher is in your life, and you are in his, for a purpose, and that purpose is always about growth and redemption. Like you, he needs grace and forgiveness as well as limits and consequences. Do not make the mistake of looking upon him as a curse to be borne or a burden to be survived.

When people ask me, "When do I give up hope on my button-pusher?" I say, "Never, as long as he is alive. Give up the demand and the requirement that he must change. But continue doing all of the things today that could make a difference tomorrow." That is the way to live in the kind of hope that God provides: "May the God of hope fill you with all joy and peace as you trust in him, so that you may overflow with hope by the power of the Holy Spirit" (Romans 15:13).

God never ceases striving, in so many different ways, to bring a difficult and wayward race to communion with himself: "I will walk among you and be your God, and you will be my people" (Leviticus 26:12). As you walk in faith to change and grow in your own life and to help your difficult person change, you are taking your place in God's grand plan and design. It is a good way to live.

May God bless you.

MAKING LIFE BETTER

1. Commit yourself to remaining in the process described in this chapter. Write out your commitment and why it matters to you.

2. Thank God now for using your button-pusher to render things down so much that you can understand what is really important in life and what can fill your life with purpose and meaning.

Notes

Chapter 2, Understand Why People Are Difficult

1. *Raising Great Kids* (Grand Rapids, Michigan: Zondervan, 1999).

2. My book *Hiding from Love* (Grand Rapids, Michigan: Zondervan, 1991) deals with this process in detail.

Chapter 4, Release What Doesn't Work

1. Henry Cloud's *Changes That Heal: How to Understand Your Past to Ensure a Healthier Future* (Grand Rapids, Michigan: Zondervan, 2003) has an excellent treatment of the splitting of grace and truth.

2. If you find that you do not choose very safe people, Henry's and my book *Safe People: How to Find Relationships That Are Good for You and Avoid Those That Aren't* (Grand Rapids, Michigan: Zondervan, 1995) explains how to discern safe from unsafe people.

Chapter 6, Invite God In

1. See *Boundaries: When to Say Yes and When to Say No to Take Control of Your Life* (Grand Rapids, Michigan: Zondervan, 1991) by Henry Cloud and me about these and other laws of relationship and responsibility.

Chapter 8, Find Others Who Are Safe and Sane

1. Safe people want the best for you, even if it means experiencing some present unpleasantness now for success in the future. See *Safe People: How to Find Relationships That Are Good for You and Avoid Those That Aren't* (Grand Rapids, Michigan: Zondervan, 1995) for more about finding safe relationships.

Chapter 12, Commit to the Process

1. For more about grief and its benefits, see chapter 11 of *How People Grow* by Henry Cloud and John Townsend (Grand Rapids, Michigan: Zondervan, 2001).

MEET DR. JOHN TOWNSEND

Dr. John Townsend is a psychologist, popular speaker, and the best-selling author and coauthor of numerous books, including the Gold Medallion Award winning, *Boundaries* and *God Will Make a Way*. He is co-host of the nationally broadcast *New Life Live!* radio program and co-founder of the Cloud-Townsend Clinic in Southern California. He holds a doctoral degree in clinical psychology from Rosemead Graduate School of Psychology at Biola University.

EMBARK ON A LIFE-CHANGING JOURNEY OF PERSONAL AND SPIRITUAL GROWTH

Dr. John Townsend has been bringing hoping and healing to millions for over two decades. As co-founder of Cloud-Townsend Resources, he as created many resources to help people discover solutions to life's most difficult personal and relational challenges.

For a complete list of all his books, videos, audio tapes, and small group resources, visit:

www.cloudtownsend.com

or call

800-676-HOPE (4673)

Cloud-Townsend Resources
Solutions for Life